Publicit
Pet Bu~~~~~~~~~

How to get visible and win media coverage

By Rachel Spencer

REVIEWS

"For most pet business owners 'getting in the paper' is only something they possibly do when they first launch their business. It can, and should be much more than that. Now, thanks to Rachel's amazing PR blueprint, any pet business owner can exploit the many media opportunities that will help position their business as the premium, expert option in their town. I will be recommending all my coaching clients grab a copy of this essential media guidebook."

DOMINIC HODGSON - GROW YOUR PET BUSINESS FAST

"Rachel is one of the most trusted journalists in the UK and when it comes to pet stories she's the person I always turn to first. She's passionate about the work she does, has great contacts and always delivers well written stories that are thoroughly researched and entertaining for our readers."

JANE ATKINSON - THE SUN ON SUNDAY

"Rachel eats, sleeps and breathes pet stories and now she's sharing what she's learned as a pet journalist so small businesses can understand how to tell theirs too. A no-nonsense guide on how to get publicity from someone with their finger on the pulse."

COLLETTE WALSH - PR AND MEDIA CONSULTANT

COPYRIGHT

Publicity Tips for Pet Businesses

Copyright © Rachel Spencer 2018

Cover Design: Amy Newlands
Interior layout: Ray-Anne Lutener

DEDICATION

For Daisy

CONTENTS

	Introduction	09
Chapter 1	How I became a pet journalist	13
Chapter 2	What is publicity?	16
Chapter 3	How publicity can help your pet business	22
Chapter 4	How being visible in the media can help you rank on search engines	28
Chapter 5	Working out what matters to you and why you started your business	35
Chapter 6	Deciding what your goals are	41
Chapter 7	How to create the right impression	49
Chapter 8	Building relationships with journalists	54
Chapter 9	Finding the right angle for your story	60
Chapter 10	How to write a pitch or press release	67
Chapter 11	What to do once you have the journalist's attention	79
Chapter 12	How to maximise your exposure	84

Chapter 13   Generating story ideas   86

Chapter 14   Social media and publicity opportunities   94

Chapter 15   When you should take out an advert   98

Chapter 16   Blogs, podcasts and working with influencers   104

Chapter 17   How having a famous pet can help your brand   117

Chapter 18   Old fashioned PR - getting yourself out there!   123

Chapter 19   How to handle a crisis   130

Chapter 20   Choosing the right PR   134

              The Final Word   141

              About the Author   144

              Acknowledgements   145

INTRODUCTION

In the ever-changing media landscape, there are so many ways to make people aware of what you do in your business.

Social media platforms like Facebook, Twitter and Instagram are fantastic for pet brands. You can publish as little and often as you like - for free!

Boosting posts means your message goes even further - paying as little as a few pounds or dollars to potentially reach thousands and, in some cases, millions of people all over the country and overseas.

Social media has made the world a smaller place and this is brilliant for pet entrepreneurs.

Rewind fifteen, even ten years ago, and this wasn't the case. Most of your customers would have been from the city, town or village where your business was based.

You might have had a website but it wouldn't have been anywhere near as sophisticated or easy to use as the one you have today.

If you wanted to share a story with your community, you'd have trawled through the local newspapers and magazines and contacted a reporter to see if they'd write about you.

So, back to where we are today. We still have local newspapers and magazines. Many of the newspapers have Facebook, Twitter and Instagram pages.

Often followers are higher than circulation figures. The Warrington Guardian - my old local paper in Cheshire where I worked in 2000 - has 64,000 followers on Facebook and sales of around 30,000.

Then there's hyperlocal websites and magazines. In Lymm for example, we have three print magazines, Lymm Life, Lymm Pages and The Essential Guide and free newspapers, the Midweek Guardian and South Warrington News, and each one has a website.

So, even in a relatively small village, there are six print titles and many other websites that people are reading every week.

I find them in the doctors and the dentist, the coffee shops and pubs and often see people sharing stories from them on my Facebook or Twitter feed.

I'm not a millennial. I'm 42, and I've worked in the print industry for 20 years so I am inclined to want to pick things up and read them.

And if I read about a pet business in a newspaper or magazine, I want to find out more. Not everyone is online and on social media, and I truly believe publicity in traditional media is still desirable.

Print isn't dead and new customers can discover you if you can find ways to feature your product or service in newspapers and magazines.

You don't need to use an expensive PR company - just a little time and creativity. I'll explain how to create your story, generate ideas, build relationships and write your own pitch and press release.

Rachel Spencer

CHAPTER ONE

How I became a pet journalist

♦ ♦ ♦

I'm a journalist and I've been working for the mainstream media since 1999.

My career began on local newspapers and I've been working for national newspapers since 2001. In 2006, I went freelance, meaning I could write about whatever I wanted to!

Work was crazy with me driving around all over the country. I'd always loved dogs and would spend as much time as I could with our family dog Charlie, a Cocker Spaniel.

Luckily, he lived nearby so I could visit for cuddles and walks whenever I liked but I always felt it wasn't fair for me to have a dog of my own, as I lived alone and traveled a lot.

Then, in 2009, it all changed. My friend Jane - a full-on crazy dog lady who re homes dogs for the RSPCA and other charities - had a baby and asked me to take care of her 'lively' terrier cross, Daisy.

Daisy was only five at the time and very full on. Anyway, Jane let me keep her and it meant I couldn't take on miserable jobs where I'd be stuck in my car all day.

Instead, I worked from home and began writing more stories about dogs. Now it's pretty much all I write about which is brilliant.

Because of this, pet brands and their PRs approach me to help with placing their clients in the press. Companies I've worked with include Royal Canin, Purina, Tails.com, FitBark, PitPat, Furbo, PetsPyjamas, LV=, Natures Menu and DogFest.

While it's great to have engaged social channels, appearing in local, regional and national newspapers and websites is desirable too.

People love to hate the Mail Online but it's the biggest newspaper website in the world. It had 12 million unique daily browsers in April 2018 - that's a lot of eyes on a brand.

My pet articles have featured in the Daily Mail, Mail on Sunday, Telegraph, Independent, The Sun, Sunday Mirror, Daily Mirror, Daily Star, Sunday People, Closer magazine, Real People, Love It magazine and BuzzFeed.

Getting coverage isn't easy - you need to be creative, come up with a unique angle and persuade an editor it will be of interest for their readers. But it can be done.

I'm a practitioner so I'm doing what I talk about in this book day in, day out and have enabled hundreds of pet companies, charities and individuals to feature in the media.

You won't find complicated theory or fluff, but simple, practical, actionable advice so you can do the same.

CHAPTER TWO

What is publicity?

♦ ♦ ♦

The Oxford English Dictionary defines publicity as: "Notice or attention given to someone or something by the media."

There's a saying that goes: "There's no such thing as bad publicity," which is associated with Phineus T Barnum of Barnum's Circus in the 19th century - most recently played by Hugh Jackman in The Greatest Showman.

Reassuringly, if you're running a pet business, unless something terrible happens to an animal in your care or who has used one of your products (I will cover this later) bad publicity is unlikely to be something you will encounter.

Understanding the media landscape

Since the digital revolution, this has completely changed.

We have the **traditional, mainstream media** like the Daily Mail, Telegraph, Guardian or the Wall Street Journal in the States.

For a traditional PR company, having a client featured in these types of publications is a huge win as it can generate masses of interest and sales.

Brands can do equally well by featuring on relatively **new media sites**, from blogs to social media and entertainment websites like BuzzFeed and LadBible.

While viral videos or photos taken by members of the public - this is known as citizen journalism - feature a lot, the more newsy content for these sites often comes from mainstream media or news agencies.

Then there are large websites like Medium and the Huffington Post. They employ trained, professional journalists and share news stories just as the mainstream media does.

Celebrities, professionals and bloggers can set up a profile on there and write posts so they are also described as social publishing platforms.

On Medium for instance, the White House has a page. So does actress Mila Kunis but you'll also find regular people like you and me, writing about taking their pets on holiday and how they coped when their beloved animal died.

With the Huffington Post, you need to be approved by their blogging team to be a contributor, but both platforms place your content in front of a different audience.

We have **regional and local media,** which would be your local weekly newspaper if you're living in a town or village, or if you're in a city, you may have a daily or evening paper.

Each reporter is given a different specialism such as politics, health or crime, and a 'patch' which is the geographical area of the city or town they cover.

As well as 'paid for' newspapers, groups publish **free newspapers or 'freesheets'** which are posted out to thousands of homes.

This could be as big as the Metro, a free newspaper given out in every city in the UK, or reach a few thousand people in a smaller community - but people still read them!

Most areas have lifestyle magazines and local news websites, sometimes described as **hyperlocal websites** which are often run by community journalists.

These are very much at the heart of the community they serve and report on stories that really matter to the people living there.

You can search for them on an interactive map at www.communityjournalism.co.uk.

For pet entrepreneurs, another place to target is **niche publications and websites**, such as Your Dog, Dogs Today, Your Cat and Pet Gazette.

Pet blogs can be useful too as their audience is pet owners. Global brands like Purina and Royal Canin work with bloggers as well as mainstream titles.

Finally, there's **social media** which is essentially your own publishing platform, so YouTube, Facebook, Instagram, Twitter, Pinterest and Snapchat.

Local and regional newspapers in particular feed stories to the nationals, and so do all the other types of sites I've mentioned. Local, regional and national newspapers all scour social media for ideas so you'll often see stories in print that started on Facebook or Twitter.

Publicity is exposure in the media for a person or a business and this guide focuses on traditional media, so local, regional and national newspapers and websites.

Appearing in or on them puts you in front of thousands, potentially millions, of people who may know nothing about you or what you do.

Being written about by an independent person - the journalist - gives you credibility as it's them, not you, who is speaking about you and your business.

It's the opposite of an advert where you are in control of the message.

CHAPTER THREE

How publicity can help your pet business

◆ ◆ ◆

How can people learn about what you do or buy your products and services if they don't know who you are?

Not everyone is on social media and while it's really important to be active and consistent on there, it's not the only way to market your business.

On Facebook, anyone can have up to 5,000 friends, join up to 6,000 groups and follow up to 5,000 pages which means they could see 15,000 posts a DAY!

The Facebook algorithm changes all the time and while you can really drill down the demographics and interests in Facebook ads to find your perfect customer, you can't guarantee they'll see it.

People aren't there to buy. They're distracted and aren't searching for products. Instead they're nosing at their friends, looking for advice and browsing for all manner of things.

But nearly every town in the UK has a newspaper, hyperlocal website and lifestyle magazine that people read because they want to learn about their community.

They need regular, interesting content to enable them to break stories and have highly engaged communities on their social medial channels.

So they're a great place for people to learn about your business.

Print isn't dead

A few years ago we kept hearing 'Print is dead.' But the truth is, it's actually having a revival.

Like vinyl (that's records for you younger readers) it's good to have something you can pick up and feel. Niche, independent magazines like Happiful and Love are doing really well.

How often do you read about something in a magazine, newspaper or website then put the name into Google and visit the brand's website or social media channels?

Personally, I do it a lot, from newspapers, websites and pet and health magazines.

I often buy whatever I've read about and sign up to mailing lists for discount codes (I am every marketer's dream!) so if you're anything like me, you'll see the value in this.

It enables you to put 'As seen on BBC Bristol' or 'As seen in the Daily Mail' on your website which looks impressive and enhances your credibility.

Whether you appear in print in a local, regional or national title, articles in newspapers and magazines are in most cases uploaded onto websites too.

Sometimes, but not always, they will include a link to your site. And these links, or people seeing your name and putting it in a search engine are key to people finding you.

Try Googling your business or name and take a look at what comes up. It shouldn't just be your website, blog and social media. You want to be able to see your business in as many places as possible.

If you have a pet business in the UK, you will be familiar with **Woof Woof Network founder Katie Tovey-Grindlay,** and here she shares how publicity helped her build her brand.

Katie set up a dog walking business in 2011 after getting Labrador puppy Bertie following a career in the Royal Navy.

After harnessing the power of social media to find clients, she recognised other pet businesses were overwhelmed by it.

She created the hugely successful Twitter chat hour #woofwoofwednesday, which runs every Wednesday 8 to 9pm UK time. and business support service Woof Woof Network, helping pet entrepreneurs.

This evolved into another online brand, Business Wonderland (www.businesswonderland.co.uk) and Katie now coaches entrepreneurs from a variety of backgrounds, from personal trainers and therapists to car manufacturers on social media.

What kind of publicity have you had with your various businesses?

When I was running my dog walking business, I was asked to appear on BBC Radio Bristol and featured in a lifestyle magazine where I live in Bristol.

The One Show contacted me through my dog walking website too, asking for help in finding dogs to film for the show.

What kind of impact did this have?

As a dog walker, I was one of many in a crowded market, but publicity elevated my reputation in my local area and made me stand out.

It showed I was an established, professional business, and speaking live on the radio made people see I was experienced and had a lot of knowledge about working with dogs.

It raised my profile and gave my business credibility.

Being in a lifestyle magazine helped me to gain more clients which is what I really wanted. People read about you, feel they know a little more about you and this helps build trust.

And you've had coverage in niche publications as well as mainstream?

Yes, with Woof Woof Network I featured on lots of online publications and blogs and blogged myself for Crufts.

I appeared in Pet Business News and the Pet Gazette and this helped give me credibility and made me more visible to people in the industry.

I wasn't looking to generate more business; it was more to raise my profile and for pet businesses to be aware of who I was and how I could help them.

You help entrepreneurs understand social media and build their online presence, how do you think traditional media fits in with this?

I think getting in front of different audiences is really important. Whether that's through newspapers, magazines or radio or guest blogs and podcasts, it all matters.

Each time you do it, you're increasing your visibility and potential to find new customers. People consume media in so many different ways so my advice is to take advantage of every opportunity.

CHAPTER FOUR

How being visible in the media can help you rank on search engines

♦ ♦ ♦

The more places people are able to see your company, the more it helps with SEO or Search Engine Optimisation.

This is important whether you have a bricks and mortar business or an online shop, and every time your website is found on the internet, the more visible you become.

Companies pay huge amounts to be at the top of search engines. Your website should be easy to use on mobile devices as we turn to our phones to find out everything.

The higher you feature on search engines and the easier you make the buying experience for customers, the more successful your business will be.

Domain Authority or DA is a score developed by an American software company called moz.com to enable companies to see how they rank on search engines and how to improve their position.

DA is calculated by looking at many factors including the number of links a website contains and the number of other sites linking to it.

A brand new website would have a DA ranking of 0 but as more people visit and other websites link to it, the higher it goes.

The DA for your own website might be low. But you can guarantee your local newspaper or hyperlocal website will have a decent DA and a national newspaper site will have a very high DA. Twitter's is 100. The Daily Mail had a score of 94 in August 2018.

You can't insist on a publication including a link if they publish an interview, press release or article about your business, but if they do, it can be helpful in building the credibility of your website with Google as **SEO expert Rosie Robinson** explains.

Rosie runs **Wuf Design** (www.wufdesign.co.uk) a website and SEO company specialising in working with pet businesses.

There are so many things for businesses to focus on, why is traditional media important?

Traditional media can easily be forgotten in amongst all the online social media channels we have today, but it can be a really positive way to extend your businesses reach especially if you have a local service business.

I like to look at marketing with a holistic view. People's user journey takes them between your website, social media, online media and traditional media. All these different formats support each other in marketing your business and reaching your potential clients and customers.

Although we may be caught up in the social media whirl, there are plenty of potential customers who still enjoy catching up with their news and local community in the more traditional manner.

If your competitors aren't marketing themselves to these people then you should definitely take the opportunity to.

Being mentioned in the press can lead to traffic to websites which is great - are there other benefits this brings?

For me it increases confidence in your brand or business and gives it authority as well.

People have a tiny attention span when surfing or searching. You have such a small timeframe to grab their attention so anything that makes you stand apart from your competition is great.

For example, if I was searching for a dog trainer in Bristol, Google would return a list of results to me with a list of dog trainers which I would scan up and down.

If there was a link to the Waggy Tails website, and also a link to an article in the Bristol Post about Waggy Tails, my brain would, in a very quick second, associate that to be a good thing, and it would increase the likelihood of me clicking on their website.

Often but not always, an online version of the article will include a backlink to the website. Why is this valuable?

Backlinks are a way of one website giving a vote of confidence to another. They're seen by Google as a positive ranking factor and can help contribute towards your own website's ranking position or search visibility.

The greater authority the website back linking to yours has, the greater weight Google will give to this.

So, a back link from a local or national press website will make more of a difference than one from your Auntie's knitting blog!

We know keeping on top of our social media, having a great website and word of mouth are ways to raise awareness of a business but being featured on a news website is evergreen content that could be there forever. What is the benefit of this?

Whilst a social media post, blog post or content share is great for promoting a particular item, product or event, it's time specific.

It's useful to the reader at that point in time and will disappear from the platform at a later date, or newer content will push it further down making it harder to see or access.

Evergreen content, so being featured in a news article online, is essentially timeless so attracts new readers and stays in the Google listings for much longer and continues to work to promote your business long after the publication date.

As an SEO expert, when people are searching for a business that has appeared on a news website compared to one that hasn't what is the difference you would expect to see?

If I was searching for the exact business name I would expect to see the company website first followed by any social media links and then a link to the article in the online press.

If I was doing a local search for a service and an area - such as 'dog walker in Hampstead' - I'd expect to see a list of businesses and usually if the business has a local press article published online that should be shown with it.

In both instances, seeing a news website link alongside the actual business website link creates trust, authority and confidence and therefore should increase your click through rate.

CHAPTER FIVE

Working out what matters to you and why you started your pet business

♦ ♦ ♦

Thinking about putting yourself out there can be daunting even though we do it every day on social media both on our personal and business pages.

Dealing with a publication, be it print or a website, is different because they tell the story the way they feel it works best.

It's not something we can control. But appearing in the media will enhance your profile and credibility and this is vital to every business.

When working with clients who have just started out, I begin with finding their 'why?'

Who are they? What are they interested in? What do they really care about? What makes them happy? What is it that drives them to do what they do? Why do they think it matters?

The answer to the final question is usually what their story is.

To demonstrate this, I went through the questions with a contact of mine, **Liz Haslam, who runs an amazing rescue for English Bull Terriers** (www.bedsforbullies.com) and I've written about her many times. She's appeared in newspapers all over the world and on TV and is a remarkable lady.

Who are you?

Liz Haslam, founder of Beds For Bullies, a charity that helps abandoned and ill-treated English Bull Terriers in the UK and worldwide.

What are you interested in?

Dogs and animal welfare.

What do you really care about?

The welfare of English Bull Terriers.

What makes you happy?

Helping English Bull Terriers, raising awareness of the breed and ensuring they have happy lives.

What is it that drives you in your work?

The abuse I have seen of English Bull Terriers is just horrific and heartbreaking and my experience of running Beds for Bullies since 2012 means I have an understanding of how to help them recover. I work with police forces to raise awareness too, which I hope will prevent other animals suffering.

Why does this matter to you?

They endure terrible cruelty that stays with them for life and I have dogs who will live their lives with me because they can't be rehomed. Their lives matter and I want them to experience the love and kindness that every dog deserves.

Can you see how Liz's final answer really captures her passion and what her rescue is all about?

The great thing about pet businesses is there is usually a really interesting story behind how they started, particularly those who come to the industry later in life.

You might have walked away from a stuffy corporate job to train wayward pups, or swapped pounding the beat as a police officer in favour of walking dogs.

Whatever it is, the first thing to fine tune is your story.

Some people find it uncomfortable talking about themselves and this is something you should try your best to overcome.

As an entrepreneur, your personality is a huge part of your brand, so try not to hide behind your products or skills.

Customers will warm to you and want to buy from or work with you - which is the end goal - if they know, like and trust you.

Think about what it is that started your journey in becoming a pet entrepreneur?

Try to make it as detailed as possible. Of course, we all love our pets, but not everyone walks away from a well paid job to set up a pet business.

So rather than talk about how qualified you are, or your amazing shop, or your sewing machine, you talk about you and explain why you do what you do.

I know if you're reading this book you're passionate about animals and this should be your focus. If someone else was describing you and what you do, what do you think they would say?

How would you describe what you do to a normal person?

Remember that you're in the pet world and will no doubt spend your time surrounded by similar people. Things that seem completely ordinary to you will be fascinating to people outside - I like to call them 'normal people.'

Take my old dog Daisy who sadly passed away earlier this year. When I'd tell 'normal people,' I bought a £180 bag to carry her around in, or spent £10 on her natural and ethically-sourced shampoo yet would grab whatever was on 2-for-1 for my own hair, or that she had £45 massages every other week, or that I tracked her steps on an activity tracker, and if I left her at home I had a £180 camera where I could watch her and give her treats, they'd say: "What?!"

We're in this pet-filled bubble and to outsiders, lots of things that go on in it are astonishing. Maybe you arrange dog birthday parties, run a pamper parlour where pets can have a pawdicure, or have a dog walking business where pooches wear trousers in the winter (all things I've written about in national newspapers) - what you do in itself is a story.

Are you doing something remarkable to help animals?

As a nation of animal lovers, we really enjoy reading heartwarming stories about them and hearing about how they improve our lives.

Likewise, we love to hear about people who are doing things to make the lives of our pets better too. If you're a behaviourist or run a walking, grooming or boarding business, that's you!

Editors are aware of the importance of our pets in our hearts and our lives and want to share stories they know their readers will enjoy.

Try answering the questions like Liz did and this will help you understand what your story is.

- Who am I?

- What am I interested in?

- What do I really care about?

- What makes me happy?

- What is it that drives me in my business?

- Why does what I do matter to me?

CHAPTER SIX

Deciding what your goals are

♦ ♦ ♦

People have all kinds of different reasons for needing publicity but these are the most common ones.

Brand awareness

If you're a new business, brand awareness will be your main focus.

Brand awareness can be built in many ways. You have your logo which encapsulates what you do and makes your business instantly recognisable.

Then there's your website and social media channels, word of mouth from your friends and family who support you, and your clients.

Brand awareness is something businesses should work on every day; on their websites, social media platforms and e-mail lists.

Reaching a specific group of individuals

When you first start your business you might have a very clear target audience.

Imagine you've created a fantastic new dog shampoo. One of your target groups would be dog groomers who would buy large bottles to use in their salon and possibly regular sized ones to sell to clients.

Another would be regular dog owners who want to use an ethically sourced product on their pet.

First, you might focus on targeting trade publications that dog groomers read so you'd research this and pitch to the relevant titles.

Next, you'd concentrate on pet owners. A good idea would be to ask people on your Facebook page which titles they read and pitch to them.

Building your business/Finding new clients

Your business may be established and you've done the hard work - telling people about who are and what you stand for - but you can't take your foot off the gas!

You don't want your customers to forget you. You want them to buy your products, use your service and be the person they turn to, so be consistent and keep showing up.

Naturally customers and clients come and go, so as an entrepreneur, you're always searching for more people to reach.

Publicity helps you gain a whole new set of eyes (or ears if radio) on your business who might not be on social media or in your social circle.

It helps you stand out in a noisy, crowded world and being written about by an independent person (the journalist) outside of your business builds trust in what you do.

Raising awareness of something your passionate about

Sharing your personal story is effective if this is your objective. A good example of this is **Jade Statt, founder of StreetVet**, (www.streetvet.co.uk) a charity set up to help homeless dogs and their owners, who I have worked with over the last year.

Jade approached me as a blogger (I was so pleased as I'd only been blogging a few months) so we had a chat and I suggested spending a day shadowing her and writing about the work she did.

I decided the best way to share Jade's story was to talk about why she came to set up StreetVet. Jade had been on a night out in London and had seen a dog with a skin condition that needed treatment but as she was off duty she was unable to help.

She realised there was hundreds of dogs in the same position, and set up StreetVet to help. At the time of writing Jade had a team of nearly 200 vets and vet nurses helping animals in London, Brighton, Bristol, Cambridge, Plymouth, Birmingham, Cheltenham and Southampton and they continue to expand.

Jade talked about what inspired her, and I interviewed and photographed two dog owners who had been helped by her team. Her personal story made it so much more powerful.

Be mindful that your objectives will change as your company grows as Jade explains.

What was your goal when you first started StreetVet?

We wanted to be able to help as many homeless people and their dogs as possible. At first, it was just my partner, Sam Joseph, and I.

I spent several months working with the Royal College of Veterinary Surgeons and registering our programme and ensuring we were complying with legislation.

Then Sam and I went out on the streets and started treating dogs. We had rucksacks with medication, food, treats and practical things like bowls and collars. Anything we could do in a regular consultation, we could do on the street.

We wanted to have vets helping animals and their owners on the streets across the UK so first, we set out to recruit vets and nurses to join us as volunteers.

How did you do this?

We launched in January 2017 and at the start, our communications work was done on social media, in vet groups on Facebook, and through our own personal networks. When people learned about what we were doing they were keen to help.

Then industry titles like Vet Times and the British Veterinary Association Website and vet support group, Vets: Stay, Go, Diversify wrote about us and by December we were working in London, Bristol and Brighton and had 50 volunteers.

What was the next stage?

Volunteers were going out and treating dogs but we needed supplies, so food, flea and worming treatment and medication.

We were all working as vets and vet nurses in different practices so we put posters up in surgeries and some of the drug companies heard about us this way or through the industry titles.

We also went to shows like Discover Dogs and the London Vet Show to be more visible. As we grew, people approached about partnering with us.

Goddard's Vets allowed us to have 10 surgeries per month, Pets Choice supplied food, The Mayhew Animal Home offered to help care for dogs and brands like Adaptil,

Thundershirt and Pet Remedy supplied products to help dogs during firework season.

You've had mainstream coverage too?

Yes, we've been in the Big Issue, Closer magazine, the Daily Mail, the Sunday Mirror, the Independent, Channel 4 and BBC news, The One Show and we appeared on Lorraine.

StreetVet relies on donations so it's important for members of the public to learn about the work we do.

In each case, we talked about why we set up StreetVet and the people we help in the hope it inspired people to support us.

Another really important message is public perception of homeless people and their dogs. People who don't appreciate the completeness of having a dog in their life might think, 'Oh, they just get one because they want people to feel sorry for them and give them more money.'

It's about making people see these dogs are loved, cherished and their needs are put before the owner.

How would you describe your communications strategy?

It evolved as we grew. We didn't have a PR person and did everything ourselves, contacting people we thought would be interested in our work at first and in time, people like The One Show and Lorraine came to us.

It was a lot of hard work and a combination of going out and meeting people, publicity, social media and word of mouth and I'm so pleased with how kind people have been and proud of what the volunteers have achieved.

CHAPTER SEVEN

How to create the right impression

◆ ◆ ◆

Consider the image you want to portray to your potential clients and how you want to present yourself.

This ties in with branding - you've got your logo on your shop front or vehicle, maybe your uniform or on your designs, but what about you?

Are you suited and booted? Or more relaxed and approachable? How do you want your customers to see you?

If you're starting out with your business, have a professional photoshoot where you decide how you want to look and get your hair and make up done professionally and if you're a bloke, get your hair cut.

Even if you go for the natural look, having this will make you feel more confident and at ease in front of the camera. I'm saying this with years of experience on shoots - it really helps.

Wear something colourful - not black - it doesn't show well in print. Ideally wear block colour or patterns and wear something fairly smart, no ripped jeans or scruffy trainers.

SMILE and look friendly. Editors don't want people pouting - unless it's a story about pouts!

Your pet should be photographed too - I'm going to give you a few examples of shots later - so make sure they're looking smart. Treat them to a groom and a new collar or harness and lead.

If you can, find a pet photographer who is used to working with animals.

Failing that, there are plenty of very affordable friendly local photographers who work with small businesses that can help you.

Ask your friends if they can suggest one, or have a look online and see their work and look for evidence that they have photographed pets.

Once you've chosen a photographer, have a think of some scenes you'd like to create and discuss this with the photographer as they will have ideas too.

For example, when I launched my pet blog, I worked with a local photographer in Lymm, Cheshire, called Jackie Tucker (www.jackietuckerphotography.com) and these were the shots I asked her to take:

Professional headshot

I wore a smart work blouse for this and trousers. It's quite formal for me but if I'm speaking to PRs or brands and they need a more professional image then this is the one I would use.

It's on my LinkedIn and my journalism social media accounts too.

Writing on my laptop

Again, in my smart work blouse, I'm typing on my laptop with some notebooks (with dogs on of course) next to me, pens and a dictaphone. This is my 'blogger' photo.

Daisy

Daisy inspired my blog and was such a brilliant poser! She did loads of shoots in the nine years I had her and was a natural. Jackie captured some gorgeous photos.

Regardless of how big a role your dog plays in your business, make sure you have a range of individual shots of them. It helps customers relate to you and you'll treasure them forever.

Daisy and I

Jackie took lot of different photos of us. Indoors, outdoors, full length, sat down, from the waist up, walking, Daisy looking up at me, me carrying Daisy and her sat on my knee. They were fab and came in lots of different shapes; square, portrait and landscape.

Finally, please, please have a photoshoot - I can't stress how important this is.

One of the things that baffles me as a journalist is when business owners don't have professional images.

Gone are the days when photographers were sent out to capture every story - most titles simply don't have the budget any more sadly.

I'm not from the selfie generation and most of us over a certain age hate having our photo taken but if you're trying to sell yourself, you need to get over this.

I interview people to help them promote what they do and they send me blurry snaps from nights out with other people on or badly cropped out and glasses of wine in their hands.

Not just start-ups. I've spoken to established brands and their pictures have been dreadful. It's the difference between getting publicity and your story ending up in the bin.

Online is so important - the paper is thrown away at the end of the week/month/day - and if you have a good selection of photos, chances are they will all be used. Think of all that SEO juice.

And finally, DON'T scrimp on the cost. It's worth investing upwards of £200 on a shoot.

You'll use these images over and over again; on your website, social media, for featured images on blog posts, in your newsletters, and when you appear in the media.

CHAPTER EIGHT

Building relationships with journalists

◆ ◆ ◆

It's so much easier to do this than it was back in 1999 when I first started out on a local newspaper - people used to come in the office and speak to you.

Now, with social media, e-mail and websites, it's simple to find the people you want to reach.

I talked about this in a Facebook group recently and some people said it felt a bit stalker-like. It's not.

Journalists are nosy people - it's why they do what they do. So it's absolutely ok to follow them.

Twitter is the preferred platform and the least intrusive. It's usually a work account for the newspaper they write for.

How do you find them?

Find out their names and don't use a general e-mail address starting with 'newsdesk' or 'editorial.' Often, they're printed on the inside page - so page two of a newspaper.

If your paper is divided into different districts, you might see the reporter's photo, phone number, e mail and Twitter handle on their district page/pages, known as their 'patch.'

In a magazine, again, there's usually a list of all the different departments. If a Twitter handle isn't on the page, do a search for their name on Twitter.

Follow all the writers and have a scan to see if any of them have photos of pets in their media album. If they do - brilliant!

You have your opportunity to connect because as an owner, they can't help but be interested in all things pet related.

Follow them, like their tweets, retweet things they share, comment and reply to them so when you contact them, they're already familiar with your name or business.

If you make products, why not send them a quick direct message and ask if it would be ok for you to send them a sample. Journalists love freebies - especially a present or treat for their pet.

If it's a service you offer it's best to wait until you have a specific pitch which could involve the writer and their pet.

But if you see something on their feed and you feel you could help them, then offer it.

So for example, they may have posted about spending four hours chasing their dog.

A behaviourist sending a direct message suggesting different ways of working on their recall would be well received. Try to always be thinking how you can solve a problem.

Social media can give you a good insight into the kind of things they're interested in, but if they don't show up on there (I would be very surprised if this is the case) and you can't find an e-mail address, call the switchboard number of the newspaper and ask them for it.

I spoke to **Gareth Dunning, Deputy Editor of the Warrington Guardian in Cheshire** to find out his advice on how pet businesses can build relationships with journalists.

How would you suggest pet business owners build relationships with local media?

It is important business owners have good relationships, whatever their background, and pet companies are generally pretty interesting.

There are lots of ways they can work with their local paper. For example, most papers these days have a Pet of The Year contest - we actually run a Pet Selfie one.

So what would be helpful for me would be if a business came forward to offer a prize or tried to get involved in some way.

Remember news desks get hundreds of emails a day. They only want the most interesting and best things, they aren't obliged to run your press releases.

So get to know them. Journalists are human too, so the more you know someone, the more they feel bad saying no when you send a story idea and the more they will want to help you out!

See if any reporters have a pet who may want to try a product or service you provide for themselves.

What kind of things do you like to hear about?

When it comes to animal stories, the more unusual they are the better.

So a pet who has beaten an awful disease, or one who has perhaps been missing for months before being found or something out of the ordinary like a new guinea pig hotel. Something readers may not have seen before.

And nothing beats human interest. People like to read about other people. So beating the odds or having a dramatic career change to work with animals and do something they're really passionate about will be well liked by readers.

What advice would you give to pet business owners about approaching you?

It is always quality over quantity. It is very unlikely your business will have something news worthy every week.

So don't send a story every week because they won't all be used and a great story you may have could be missed.

Images are important so always ensure you have good quality, high resolution photos to accompany your story or press release and video too if possible.

Think about when you go online or buy a paper yourself. What do you like to read? What catches your eye?

It is those ingredients news editors and reporters want as well. So look for the best picture or something that will make a good headline.

Not many papers have their own photographer these days so think about providing a great picture. This means it is far more likely your piece will be used.

What's the most interesting story you've covered from a pet business owner?

My favourite was one about a guinea pig hotel near Lymm. It is a glammed up kennel complete with gourmet food, luxury bedding and even special rooms where the pets can have some 'alone time' with their favourite holiday friends.

I also enjoyed a story this week of a woman who gave up a career in the care industry to launch her own business to pamper pets, getting people with autism to help out.

She also had a cute dog called Elf who was the face of the firm so that meant we had nice, engaging photos to use alongside the story too.

CHAPTER NINE

Finding the right angle for your story

♦ ♦ ♦

This may sound brutal but when you're considering how you're going to feature in the publication imagine you're the editor.

They're going to be thinking: "Why would our readers care about this?"

First, make sure you read the publication thoroughly. Look at the different sections in there and think about where you could see yourself.

Most papers have business and district pages and often a lifestyle section profiling interesting people, places, businesses and events of interest to the local community.

Then try to imagine different ways your story might feature but always be mindful that your story must be interesting. Then ask yourself, 'Why would this matter to the reader?'

One way to gauge what is interesting is looking at your story idea or angle as an extension of your social media. Think about your most engaging posts.

When I was working in newsrooms, we used to refer to a good story as a 'talker.' This is the kind of story people would talk about in the pub, so something we knew would go down well with our readers.

The modern equivalent of this is a story that might be shared on social media. Newspapers want shareable content on their platforms like everyone else and pet stories do well online.

According to research by Statista; in 2018, 45 per cent of people in the UK owned a pet; with a quarter having a dog and nearly a fifth a cat, so pet stories are very relatable.

Whether you make bandanas, bow ties or collars and leads for dogs, or you're a behaviourist who can turn the most troubled rescue dog into a treasured family pet, people will always want to hear about what you do.

Here's a few examples of the kind of stories that would get an editor's attention.

"I gave up my job as a PE teacher to set up a boot camp for dogs."

This was an interview I did with **Jo Cottrell who founded Dog Trouble** (www.dogtrouble.co.uk) in 2007 to rehabilitate problem dogs and to teach owners how to understand them better.

She is a truly remarkable lady who has saved the lives of hundreds of dogs and works with rescue centres giving dogs a second chance.

Jo's inspiring story appeared in the Sunday Mirror.

"How your pet can have their own personal shopper."

I did this feature with Pet London (www.petlondon.net). How many pet boutiques are there? You can find one on many high streets.

But rather than go on about the shop, we talked about the personal shopping experience and Daisy was styled by Rebecca.

It made a fun story with great photos and appeared in the Sunday Mirror and Daily Mail.

"Dog groomer helps rescue dogs find fur-ever homes."

This story was in my local paper, the Warrington Guardian. Dog groomer Jenny Jones was opening a new salon, Scizzor Yappy. That story would only have made about a paragraph.

Instead, she spoke about how she set up her business to help dogs and how she was giving free grooms to pups at a rescue centre to help them find homes.

It was the main story on Page 3 - which is one of the most read places in any newspaper. You can see how much more interesting this was than, 'woman opens grooming salon.'

For the lowdown on how to create a great story, I spoke to **Jane Common, Pets Editor at Real People magazine.**

Jane writes heartwarming, funny and quirky stories from the UK and worldwide and receives hundreds of pitches and press releases every week.

Jane also has a travel blog for pets, (www.PhilleasDogg.com) sharing her dog Attlee's advice on places to go and a book, Philleas Dogg's Guide to Dog Friendly Holidays in Britain and you can follow her on Twitter and Instagram @janecommon.

What kind of stories do you like to hear about for your pet page?

Our Animal Crackers page features one long real life read a week – so an owner telling us about their pet who's remarkable in some way. (Of course, all pets are remarkable in one way or another!)

We've featured a parrot who chatted to his owner's Amazon Alexa and ordered some cake stands; fat cats who've become super-slimmers (and even a dieting hamster); dogs who've got into scrapes including getting stuck down a rabbit hole and falling off a cliff (all with happy endings, of course) and inspiring stories of dogs and cats who have diagnosed their humans' cancer or bravely battled ill health of their own.

One of my favourite stories was about the first cat in Britain to have a pacemaker fitted and this week I'm writing about a 48-year-old tortoise who's looking for love.

What's the most interesting story you've covered from a pet business owner?

I'm working on a story at the moment about a lady who runs a dog grooming salon and dyed her own dog pink for her wedding day!

We've featured women whose pets have inspired their businesses – a lady whose dog had allergies, for example, which she cured by baking her own dog biscuits.

I've also interviewed dog trainers who have worked with assistance dogs about the amazing impact they can have on people's lives.

Is there anything else that could help with publicity for pet companies?

Yes, every week there's a slot called 'Get Me One' in which we feature a pet-related product – toys, treats, food, beds and blankets... everything under the sun really.

The most bizarre we've published was a toy cannon for guinea pigs!

What advice would you give to pet business owners looking to gain coverage?

Read the magazine before pitching and tailor your approach accordingly – the amount of pitches I receive from people who have clearly never read Real People is staggering.

Think about your products but also whether there is a real life or human interest story attached to your business.

If your cat goes to work every day with you, that's interesting. Engage with editors and writers who are interested in pets on social media.

If anybody emails me and knows my pets' names (Attlee the dog and Dodger the cat, both stars of my Instagram account) then I'm impressed and more likely to be amenable to a conversation.

CHAPTER TEN

How to write your pitch or press release

♦ ♦ ♦

Journalists receive hundreds of emails a day from people asking them to feature their story, brand or service so how do you ensure your message stands out? The good news is you don't need to hire a PR firm - YOU are the best person to tell your story.

What 20 years of writing for local, regional and national newspapers as both a staff reporter and a freelance journalist has taught me is that it's about telling great stories that are relevant to the readers of the publication you're targeting.

First, do your research. Reporters on local titles look for stories that people in their community will care about. If they cover a council estate, they won't want to read about hedge funds.

You should have already found the person who is most likely to be interested in your story by following the advice in **Chapter Eight - Building relationships with journalists**.

If you're pitching to a national journalist or a freelance, before you start, research what kind of stories they cover and make sure they write about your industry.

I get hundreds of emails every day about things I have never written about.

Today for example, I have press releases about office ergonomics, bitcoins, farm to face skincare, making a will, school backpacks and turtles in the Seychelles.

They go in the bin because I write about the pet industry. I love writing human interest stories about people doing remarkable things to help animals and doing extraordinary things for them. They're the people I want to hear from.

Take Jenny Jones from Scizzor Yappy who I mentioned earlier. If she'd hired a PR to send a press release about how she was opening a shop, I'd have deleted it.

But if she sent me an e-mail saying she was helping rescue dogs find forever homes by giving them free grooms, I would have been hopping up and down in excitement at her story.

So you don't have to send out a press release. If you have a brilliant story, just a few lines on e-mail will do.

How to write an e-mail pitch:

1. Use the subject line as your headline.

Think about where your story might appear in the paper, so if it's for a business section, start with 'Business Story', if it's covering a particulate district, say, a village named Stretton, use 'Stretton Story,' or if they do a Tried and Tested page, it would be 'Tried and Tested Idea.'

2. Explain succinctly what the story is about.

If you're launching a pampering package for pets and their owners, the title of your e-mail should read something like this.

'Tried and Tested Idea: Beauty salon launches spa day for dogs and their owners'.

3. Get to the point.

Avoid a long introduction. You have seconds to get the reporter's attention. For this story, I'd say something as simple as this.

'I run Fuss Salon in Stretton and I was wondering if you might be interested in a story about our spa days for dogs and their owners.'

4. Be friendly and enthusiastic.

Imagine how many serious, stuffy, corporate emails they get a day and be the opposite. Let them know a little about you.

Write as you would if you were telling a great story to someone in the pub - it's ok to be excited and sound passionate about what you do!

5. Create a 'call to action.'

You want to hear back from the reporter, so create a strong call to action. In this instance, I would invite them to try out the pampering package themselves and ask them to call or e mail to arrange it.

Newspapers and magazines love tried and tested features with reporters getting up to all kinds of weird and wonderful things.

6. Send a photo to illustrate the story.

Attaching a photo of a dog and their owner sitting side by side being pampered in a beauty salon would help sell this story in.

The reporter can see the scenario themselves and it would make a fun, engaging image to use in the paper. Only send one or two small images.

The final pitch should be:

Tried and Tested Idea: Spa days for dogs and their owners launched at beauty salon

Hi (Name of reporter)

I'm Helen, a beauty therapist from Fuss Salon in Stretton and I was wondering if you might be interested in a story about our spa days for dogs and their owners.

The dogs have a full wash and blow dry, a blueberry facial, their nails clipped and there is an option to have them painted with pet friendly nail polish! The humans have a facial, blow dry and manicure and they sit side by side throughout the treatment.

I'm a dog owner myself and I love pampering my Cockerpoo Daisy and had the idea after having a doggy pamper party at home with a few of my friends and their dogs. They loved it and said I should offer it at the salon.

If you'd like to try the service yourself with your dog we would absolutely love to welcome you to Fuss. I've attached a photo so you can see how it works!

I look forward to hearing from you soon,

Many thanks, Helen

Fuss Salon was founded in 2005 by beauty therapist Helen and hairdresser Joanne, who trained together at Stretton Beauty College. Find out more at www.yourwebsite.co.uk or call (your phone number).

What is a Press Release and why should I send one?

In the Oxford Dictionary of Journalism, Tony Harcup defines a press release as 'Information sent to the media by or on behalf of individuals or organisations seeking to publicise an announcement, product, event, policy, campaign or anything for which they hope to attract coverage.

'A press release will often be written in the form of a ready-made news story complete with quotes but journalists are trying to treat such material as merely the start of a potential story rather than the end.'

Thanks to huge budget cuts in the industry because of falling advertising revenue and the never-ending demand for online content, we see less of the skepticism he refers to in the second part of the description.

A very well written, targeted press release could be cut and pasted and put on a page or online, so they are an effective way to get coverage.

Publications need a variety of stories, so a press release about a new staff member or an award might make a very short story or 'nib' which stands for 'news in brief' on a business or community page.

Or something more fun and quirky could make a page lead - the main story on a page.

The press release should give the reporter all the information they need so they can decide if it's a story they want to pursue.

Let's say your pet shop is celebrating being open a year and you want the local paper to cover it.

Your dream scenario is that you write a press release and send it to the reporter you know has a dog, and invite them to a 'pool pawty' you're organising to mark the event which is going to raise money for a local animal shelter.

They write a story before the event, telling owners they can attend, then cover the event itself and if you're really lucky, they might send a photographer. If not, no problem, because it's going to be so eye catching you hire a photographer to cover it yourself.

How to write a Press Release:

You want your press release to read like a story so before you start, look at the tone and style of the publication and try to emulate it.

Think of the 'Five Ws' which are who, when, where, why and what and how. These are the essential questions that should be answered in every story.

Following the Five Ws is taught to reporters at journalism college. They write a story assuming the reader has no prior knowledge of anyone involved in it so include as much detail as possible. My tutors would say: "Imagine your reader has landed from Mars!"

- A press release should be between 250 and 400 words long.

- At the top, write NEWS RELEASE or PRESS RELEASE in capital letters and centre.

- Place your headline below: Pool party for pups to raise funds for Stretton Animal Shelter

- Add the date and 'For immediate release.'

- Write your 'Intro' or introduction. This should tell the story in one short sentence and be around 15-25 words long.

- Follow with two paragraphs explaining the story in more detail and introducing the person who the story is about.

- Add two or three sentences with direct quotes explaining why the story is important, who is involved and how it came about.

- Provide more background information and explain how people can get involved. This should be one or two sentences.

- Include another quote from the person in the story, or another organisation who affected by what happening in the story, in this case, the dog shelter. Finish the story with a strong call to action, telling the reader what to do next, such as find out more visit yourwebsite.co.uk or add an e-mail contact address you@yourwebsite.co.uk

- Write ENDS in capital letters, which tells the reporter the story has finished.

- Include an Editors Notes section, giving any further information the reporter might need, so who to contact, details about the people/organisations involved.

This is an example of a press release I did for a charity event organised by a contact who runs an artisan pet business.

HEADLINE: Dog lovers urged to join in mass walkies event to raise funds for children's charity

DOG owners in Altrincham are invited to what hopes to be the town's biggest ever walk to raise month for the Children's Adventure Farm Trust.

Rob Benson who runs pet stall B&V Trading on Altrincham Market has teamed up with his trader colleagues to raise money for the charity.

The Mooch With Ya Pooch event will take place on Sunday May 21st, with walkers meeting at 10.30am before the walk starts at 11am at John Leigh Park. Entry is £10 and all proceeds go to CAFT.

Rob said: "The Children's Adventure Farm Trust does such an important job for children and their families in the North West and we wanted to do something to help.

"I meet so many dog walkers at the market and we thought a sponsored dog walk would be something for all the family to enjoy and raise money for this fantastic cause.

"My colleagues at Alty Market loved the idea when I told them and pledged their support too, so we want Mooch With Your Pooch to be the biggest dog walk ever in Altrincham."

Walkers can choose from three different routes and each one finishes at Altrincham Market House between 11.30am and 12.30pm.

Every pet will get a doggy bag filled with treats, a Canines for CAFT balloon and rosette plus entry for one dog to the dog show, which takes part from 1.30pm.

Jure Modic from CAFT said: "This will be a real community effort and we're so grateful to everyone involved in putting it all together, especially Rob and everyone at Altrincham Market who have worked so hard to make it all possible.

"The money raised will help us to provide life-changing holidays here at the Adventure Farm for terminally ill, disabled and disadvantaged children from our region.

"We really can't thank everyone enough for their support, together we can make a real difference in the lives of these very special children."

To find out more or book a place, pick up a form from Altrincham Market or contact Rob@yourbusiness.co.uk

Ends

Editors Notes:

B&V Trading was established in 2017 and provides hand made pet accessories and artisan treats. Owner Rob Benson lives in Altrincham with his Dalmation Cotton and Dachshund Vivienne. Rob can be reached on rob@yourbusiness.co.uk or 01234 56789.

CAFT was founded in 1985 and is based at Booth Bank Farm and provides activities and holidays for disabled, terminally ill and disadvantaged children and their families across the North West.

Attach one low resolution photo and let the journalist know more high resolution pics are available and, ideally, put images in a Dropbox or WeTransfer link so they have the option to download them.

Your press release should contain all the information the reader requires and give the journalist everything they need to write the story plus contact details for everyone involved in case they have any questions.

CHAPTER ELEVEN

What to do once you have the journalist's attention

♦ ♦ ♦

Don't panic! If a reporter responds to your e-mail this is brilliant.

You should have everything clear in your mind that you want to say, plus your pictures and it's key to be as helpful and accommodating as possible.

Ideally the reporter will want to speak to you. If they can meet you, that really is amazing. But chatting on the phone is just as good.

Don't offer to reply to questions on e-mail. Reporters want to speak to people and you will get a much better feature by having a conversation.

It's a good idea to jot down the key messages you want to get across beforehand but try to introduce them naturally into the conversation so you sound like a person, not a robot.

They don't want to hear a load of corporate sounding nonsense or jargon. Avoid bizarre or overly important sounding job titles and keep things simple.

Often the golden nugget that really makes a story comes from out of the blue as you chat. Something an interviewee doesn't consider very interesting or just takes for granted can be fascinating to other people.

For example, I went to the Purina Better With Pets Forum in Barcelona in June 2018 where five social entrepreneurs who were using the harnessing the power of dogs to make lives better were pitching for a £75,000 prize.

Two were from the UK; Medical Detection Dogs (www.medicaldetectiondogs.co.uk), and Canine Hope (www.canine-perspective.com), an enterprise where rape survivors and rescue dogs work together to help each other recover.

I interviewed Claire Guest from Medical Detection Dogs about a new project where her dogs were helping to diagnose Parkinson's Disease.

Claire told me that her own father John had been diagnosed and this was what inspired her to see if dogs could sniff out the disease.

The story about the dogs working with Parkinson's UK had been covered extensively, but Claire's first hand experience of seeing how it affected her family meant it was covered again.

In the press release I had been sent about the event there was no mention of this. But by interviewing Claire, I was able to find a fresh angle and wrote an engaging, human interest story about the importance of the work to Claire and her family.

When you speak to the reporter, be friendly, be interesting and remember they are human too. It's unlikely they'll ask you anything you really don't want to answer but if they do, be polite and simply say, 'Would you mind if I took a little time to think about that?'

I asked journalists in my network to share their tips for interviewees.

"Make sure you've read the title before, Have a clear message and give detail where appropriate and don't be monosyllabic."

"I've done a few interviews recently where halfway through they've said, 'This is off the record but...'. Of course, if you say something and then realise you shouldn't have said it then try and see if they're willing to leave it out but if something pops into your mind that you want to be 'off the record,' just don't say it."

"If you're doing a phone interview, make sure you're in a quiet room with little echo."

"Don't ask at the end of the interview for them to send you a copy of the article to approve!"

"Have an opinion. And be chatty. Nothing worse than an interview that feels like pulling teeth."

"Be a soundbite machine. Try to say something quotable, because that's what the journo is after."

"Say things with actual meaning. I recently spoke to an 'entrepreneur' whose business was all about 'assisting clients in the creation and development of deliberate business.' Even when I kept asking him to simplify he couldn't and I had no idea what his business even was."

"Understand your rights - you don't have the right to read any copy before it's printed, you don't have the right to change words and phrases you might not like. If you are a details person and in a 15 minute phone call you share 2,000 words, be prepared that those details will be summarised and it's not 'wrong' to leave things out. If this really bothers you - choose a few salient points and stick to them."

Remember, ultimately, you want it to be a pleasant experience for both of you and the more helpful you are, the more likely they are to contact you again.

CHAPTER TWELVE

How to maximise your exposure

♦ ♦ ♦

So the story comes out - now it's your chance to make the most of it.

Make sure you put it on your website. If you have a news/press section this is the ideal place for it and put 'As seen in XX' on your homepage. If you contact the publication to see if you can use their logo, they may charge you.

If you run a service business or a pet friendly holiday cottage and the writer is talking about their experience, you might want to include it in a review or testimonial section.

Follow the publication on all their social media channels, and post the piece there. If it's print, take a photo and post something along the lines of 'We're thrilled to be in @nameofpublication talking about how we…. thank you @reporter, it was great working with you.'

It's likely the publication will share the post or retweet it, and the reporter, so it reaches three different audiences - your own, the title, and the writer's.

Think of a series of social media posts to share over the next week or month. You might use a quote from the piece or one of the images to share different posts.

Finally, thank the reporter. Being a journalist is often described as a 'thankless task,' and honestly, I am always so moved when people say thank you.

It really does mean a lot and all it takes is a quick e-mail. Better still, send a card and you will stick in their mind.

CHAPTER THIRTEEN

Generating story ideas

♦ ♦ ♦

So you've had your first 'hit' or story - well done. You've started to build a relationship with the reporter.

The next step is to continue your good work. As Gareth says, you don't want to be badgering them every week, but reporters value good contacts.

They make their lives easier, so to become one of the names they want to see in their inbox, you need to start thinking like a journalist and generating story ideas.

Features can be planned weeks or months in advance.

If you've built up a relationship with a reporter, you can contact them to ask what their deadlines are for Christmas gift guides or if they have any features planned that you could help with.

It means you don't miss out and by offering something useful to include in their feature, you're helping them too. So think ahead, particularly if you make products and can work on themes.

Don't be disheartened if you don't hear back from every pitch or idea you send. Forward planning is a good habit to get into. You probably already do it for your social media posts.

If you get into the routine of generating ideas, even if they're not picked up, you can repurpose them as a blog post on your website and in your newsletters.

Here you'll find some of the most common ones to help you brainstorm.

Pages/Sections

Have a look through the paper or magazine and take a note of the different pages or sections they run every week.

My local paper has district pages reporting news from different areas, so if I was trying to place a story about a charity event in Lymm, I would pitch it to the reporter who covered that page. Then, you know you're targeting people in that area.

It has a business page with stories about start ups, companies who have won awards and businesses sponsoring community projects.

There's a lifestyle section which focuses on culture, food, music, films, gardening and travel and a pet of the week section.

Some papers have regular slots like 'A day in the life,' 'Five minutes with,' 'It happened to me,' or 'Life lessons,' where people share their knowledge and experience.

Think of how your business could fit into one.

Events in the calendar

These are days that are set in stone every year, so Christmas, Easter, Valentine's Day, Mother's Day, Halloween, Bonfire Night, Easter and New Year.

Here's some examples of articles a pet business could feature in.

Gift guides

Most papers will separate gift guides into sections at Christmas, looking at gifts for mums, dads, grandparents, kids and because pets are part of the family, they feature too.

I've placed a pet themed Valentine's Day feature in a national newspaper with gifts for pets and pet owners, so it would do you no harm at all to send over a press release or sample of a Valentine's themed product.

Pet health advice

Christmas and Easter create all kinds of hazards for pets Trees, lights, decorations, chocolate, drunk relatives can all be harmful.

If you're a dog walker, sitter, trainer or behaviourist you are qualified to give advice on how to keep pets safe.

Don't get me started on Bonfire Night and New Year. If you provide products to help pets keep calm, readers need to hear about them.

Compose a brief e-mail outlining your story idea, who you are and what your advice is.

Awareness days

Is there an Awareness Day that's really relevant to your business? There are so many that I would only pitch if it's very specific.

Earlier this year I was really impressed to see dog photographer Kerry Jordan create her own - National Dog Photography Day on July 26. The hashtag went viral and the story was picked up by newspapers in the UK, Ireland and America, so it was brilliant for Kerry's photography business (www.whippetsnippets.co.uk)

Kerry gave tips on how to take photos of dogs too and achieved fantastic coverage.

News peg

As a journalist on a local paper, you look at what's going on in the national news and try to find a local angle or peg that's relevant to readers.

During the 2018 World Cup, the Warrington Guardian ran features on Jesse Linghard because he'd grown up in the town. While everyone was talking about the football, Jesse was from the town, so of huge interest to his very proud community.

As a business owner, you can do the same. Watch the news, read the papers and industry titles and get Google alerts and think about the stories that are trending and whether they give you an opportunity to talk about your brand.

Say you're a behaviourist. In 2018, the Kennel Club announced French Bulldogs had overtaken Labradors as the most popular breed in the UK so you could write about the things potential owners need to consider.

Here's your pitch.

To: Reporter

From : You

Title: PITCH: What people in (town/village) need to know about French Bulldogs

Hi (insert name of reporter)

I'm a dog trainer in (where you live) and I wondered if you would be interested in a piece about French Bulldogs and what people need to know about the breed.

This week it was announced they had overtaken Labradors to be the most popular breed in the UK. Sadly many are handed over to rescues as people adopt them with little knowledge of their needs.

I wondered if I could write an article explaining what people need to know; their personalities, the health issues that affect them, their exercise requirements and what makes an ideal home for a Frenchie.

I feel this would promote responsible pet ownership and enable readers to make an informed decision whether a French Bulldog is the right dog for them, and support the work of rescue centres too.

Thanks for taking the time to read this and I look forward to hearing from you.

Many thanks,

Your name, contact number.

Or if you're an accessory brand you could create a story from a recent survey by American Express that found owners spend £540 a year on treats and accessories.

You could make this story your own by talking about the trends you've seen in your business - and share cute photos of pets in their purchases.

Here's how you'd pitch it:

To: Reporter

From: You

Subject: PITCH: How pets in (area) are becoming furry fashionistas

Hi (insert name of reporter)

I wondered if you might be interested in a feature on how fashion conscious pets are in (area).

A recent survey by American Express found owners spend £540 a year on treats and accessories.

I make accessories for pets and found in the last year there has been a 25% increase in pets wearing bowties, 34% increase in bandanas and 45% increase in coats.

I have photos of pets dressed in their accessories and have attached a selection. If you or any colleagues have a dog and would like to try any items, please take a look at our website to see the full range and we would be happy to gift them.

Thanks for taking the time to read this and I look forward to hearing from you.

Many thanks,

Your name, contact number.

Reporters won't expect to hear from a pet business every week. Instead, sit down with your calendar and plan ahead just as you might with your social media posts.

I would suggest doing this every quarter. Pinpoint key dates where you feel you can offer something of value to readers and build ideas around them.

CHAPTER FOURTEEN

Social media and publicity opportunities

◆ ◆ ◆

Social media is a huge part of marketing your pet business and it can present loads of publicity opportunities.

On Twitter, take a look at the hashtags #prrequest #journorequest #casestudy #bloggerrequest and you'll see what I mean.

Follow accounts that have #journorequest in their bio too.

Journalists are always appealing for people to interview for stories from all kinds of different backgrounds.

Women's magazines in particular love inspiring and quirky stories and as a pet business owner you're perfectly placed to provide these.

A feature I've written over and over again is people who go from one career to a very different one, or even who combine two jobs that you wouldn't usually put together.

One example was a lady who worked in a clothes shop during the daytime and as a fire eater in the evenings. Her story appeared in a national newspaper and women's magazine.

'Mumpreneur' stories are very popular. So if you make dog biscuits in between school runs or create beautiful pet accessories while juggling busy family life, keep an eye out for journalists looking to speak to women like you.

In some cases, you might be sharing a more personal story about yourself where mentioning your business is a small part of it.

Case study requests which focus on careers are fantastic opportunities to speak about your business and to take out an advert for the same amount of editorial space would cost hundreds if not thousands of pounds.

You might spend lot of time on social media - if that's the case then try to check these hashtags a couple of times a day.

If you can't get online so often, take a look when you have a spare moment.

Make sure you follow all the newspapers, magazines and websites in your local area on each social media platform and try to engage when you can.

Reporters may ask for people to talk about certain topics so again, this is a great way to get you and your business featured.

Your profile should be optimised so if people are searching for businesses in your niche they can find you - including journalists.

Vicky Gunn runs Millie's Beach Huts in Essex and Suffolk and regularly uses the #beachhut hashtag and has it in her Twitter bio. When the Mail on Sunday were researching a story on the best beach huts to visit in the UK, they found her and she had a fantastic piece of free publicity.

There's an excellent Facebook Group I'd recommend joining called Feature Me! run by two former Daily Mail journalists, Sadie Nicholas and Jill Foster where opportunities are posted daily.

Two of my contacts, James Roberts of Progressive Travel Recruitment and Helen Pritchard of Helen Pritchard Online, gave comment in an article on millennials where they were able to position themselves as experts in their field and mention their brand.

My favourite feature from this page is 'My dog weighs more than me!'

One of my contacts is Mark Sanders who runs www.montydogge.com and he kindly put me in contact with a lady with two Newfoundlands, Murphy and Molly who weighed 12 and 10 stone respectively.

The woman didn't have a pet business - but if she did this would have been a great chance to gain exposure in a fun and engaging way.

CHAPTER FIFTEEN

When you should take out an advert

◆ ◆ ◆

This book was inspired by a post on Facebook in a support group I'm in called The Barking Tribe for Pet Entrepreneurs - if you're not already in it, look it up!

One posted that she'd been approached by a huge glossy fashion magazine to see if she'd like to take out an advert.

The fee was £500 and she had only launched her business making gifts and accessories for pets and their owners and hampers.

People in the group responded. A few had taken out the same advert, and appeared in a two page advertorial alongside 30 other products.

Each had a photo of a product and a large paragraph - about three sentences - about their business and their website address. Some had prices and discount codes. All were 'luxury' but not all of them were for pets.

Those who had paid £500 said it was great to be able to put 'As seen in *Glossy Fashion Mag*' on their website, but didn't see a huge spike in sales, and that it was a LOT of money that could have been better spent.

It's easy to be dazzled by the prospect of appearing in a magazines that are read by potentially millions of people.

But think about what they're interested in. Only a very small number of glossy fashion mag readers will be looking for things for their pet. They're more interested in clothes and beauty.

If the post had been about advertising in a dog magazine, my feelings would have been different. There, readers are looking for things to buy their pet. It's targeted and a chance to reach people all over the UK so it's a much better investment.

There are times when you should take out an advert - when it's imperative that you reach people. I'd combine this with social media advertising as well and ensure you're targeting your ideal customer.

So for example, you're hosting a charity dog show. You'd put it on your website, e-mail your mailing list, tweet about it, make a poster/graphic and share on Facebook and Instagram and go into ads manager and target a campaign to reach the kind of people you'd like to attend.

But you want to make sure you get as many people there as possible and lots of your supporters might be elderly, so not necessarily on social media.

Taking out an advert in your local paper or magazine to tell them about the event means you know you have it covered so you'd decide when people need to see it, contact the advertising team and ensure it goes in the right edition.

I'd also contact the editorial team and tell them about it as there's every chance they would write a small piece about a charity event. But they can't guarantee it will appear. Pages change right up to the point where they're sent to the printers, and if your story gets pulled, you miss out on that chance to share your message.

If you'd like your business to feature in a lifestyle magazine, in some cases you have to take out an advert. Some only feature their advertisers, but this can be worthwhile. If you buy an advert - and they're more reasonably priced - you're usually offered an 'ad feature' or 'advertorial' too. If you're not, then ask for one as part of the package.

This is where you get a chance to talk about your business and it can be a single or a double page feature with photos. It's called an 'advertorial' as it should blend in with the rest of the articles in the magazine and is written in a journalistic style, so it doesn't look like an advert.

However, unlike an editorial piece, you should get the chance to approve the content and the layout of the page.

Some magazines employ journalists or freelancers to interview business owners and write advertorials, and if this is the case, please follow the advice I've given in **Chapter 5: Working out what matters to you and why you started your business.** Prepare for the interview. Think about what drives you and be interesting. This is your chance to really shine and engage people. Don't be boring!

If they ask you to submit content yourself, don't worry. Follow the tips in **Chapter 10: How to write your pitch or press release.** Ask what the word limit is and take time to craft a feature that will interest people in you and your business. Choose which of your professional, high resolution photos you'd like to use.

Visualise how you want the feature to appear. Do you have any customers who could provide a testimonial? Can you provide tips for pet owners? Here is a chance to create a really interesting feature.

Here's an example. Sally is a dog trainer, so the main article will be about her and why she became a dog trainer. She'll talk about her own dog/dogs and their personalities, the challenges she faces, why owners can benefit from having expert advice and anything she feel passionate about, such as reward based training.

Then she could have a 'box' - this is a separate area to the main story which breaks up the page and makes it easier to read - with a testimonial or case study, which would read something like this.

Sarah asked me to help with her dog Scamp. He'd been in a shelter for six months and was reactive when approached by other dogs. We (explain what you did to overcome this succinctly) and after XX months he became a calm, well adjusted dog.

Sarah said: "I was so worried about Scamp and walks were so stressful for both of us. The thought of returning him to the rescue was unbearable. Sally was so patient with him and helped him understand how to behave around other dogs. She continues to support us and Scamp is now a friendly, well adjusted dog."

See how engaging it is? Here Sally has someone else telling readers how she solved a problem, but not giving the big sell.

Sally might want to write another box on 'Five tips for people adopting a rescue dog' to show her expertise and provide a helpful resource for potential new clients, plus a link to her website and social media channels for people to follow.

Advertising can be costly but if you do your research and it results in a lovely article in a publication your potential customers read, it can be a good investment. If your business is making luxury dog beds, for example, a feature in an interiors magazine could be really lucrative.

CHAPTER SIXTEEN

Blogs, podcasts and working with influencers

♦ ♦ ♦

Being featured in a newspaper or magazine is impressive, but blogs and podcasts can help you reach clients particularly if they focus on your niche - pets.

Blogs

There are millions of blogs out there. As of June 2018, Tumblr alone hosted 360 million and globally 50,000 are launched per day on Wordpress.

Before working with a blogger, do your research. Media organisations like Vuelio who connect PRs with media outlets compile lists of Top 10 bloggers or bloggers to follow.

Or you could simply ask your audience on Facebook or Twitter which pet blogs they follow or enjoy.

Once you've found a blogger who you feel is the right fit consider your pitch. Why should they write about you?

Would you like them to review your product? Share your personal story? Can you offer something that is of real value to their readers?

Some bloggers will review products in exchange for being gifted an item, or write a travel piece in exchange for a stay. If you offer a unique service they will (or they certainly should) want to try it for themselves.

Don't be surprised if they ask about budget or if you are looking for a 'sponsored post.' In most cases they aren't being cheeky.

Many blog professionally, dedicating time and effort to crafting posts, taking images and sharing their work on social media.

Ask for their media kit which should tell you what their blog's Domain Authority or DA is (as explained in Chapter Four), how many visitors they have each month, the demographic of their readers, so their age, gender, location and testimonials from people they've worked with.

Make sure you read other reviews and sponsored posts to get a feel of how they write and work.

Personally, I feel the more frank and honest a blogger is, the better. How much detail do they go into? Do they talk about positives and negatives? Do they use lots of photos?

I would steer clear of working with people who write fluff such as 'I went here and it was nice,' or who are testing a different kind of dog food every month - it's not fair on their pet.

If you decide to collaborate, put together some terms and conditions.

It can be something as simple as 'I BRAND agree to pay BLOGGER £150 for INTERVIEW/REVIEW of PRODUCT plus one Facebook post, one Instagram post and three Tweets and the amount will be paid XX days after publication.'

Finally, once the blog comes out, thank the blogger and make sure you share it on your social media channels too.

Great things can come from featuring on blogs

In May 2017, I started a pet blog, www.thepawpost.co.uk. because I wanted to write about things that really mattered to me.

It's a mix of reviews, news, travel features and health stories but the ones I enjoy the most are human interest stories about people doing extraordinary things for animals.

Often they'll be stories that might be difficult to place in a newspaper or magazine, or that I feel warrant more space (most newspaper stories are between 250-800 words.)

Some of the stories have led to people appearing in other newspapers and on TV and radio.

I did an interview with Liz Haslam, founder of Beds For Bullies, aiming to help her rescue find a new home.

She talked about the 16 dogs living with her who can't be rehomed - all such heartwarming stories - and well wishers donated £2000 to ease her financial pressures.

The story was picked up by a news agency and appeared in several national newspapers and she was invited to talk about her work on ITV's This Morning.

When my dog Daisy was diagnosed with dementia in January 2018, I wrote a piece aiming to help other owners if their pet was diagnosed. Educating owners on how to care for our senior dogs is something I feel very passionately about.

Dementia affects 68% of dogs over 15 and as part of the feature, I mentioned a support group for owners, caringforaseniordog.com run by a lady called Hindy Pearson.

One of my old journalism college friends, Simon Hoban, who works for the BBC, saw it and said Radio 2 would like to do a piece on it.

Hindy gave an interview about her dog Red, who has sadly since passed away, helping to raise awareness of the condition and the support she provides to millions of listeners.

While featuring on a small blog might not have the initial appeal of a larger website or publication, these examples show that you just don't know who might pick up on it.

Podcasts

Being interviewed on a podcast is a great way to express your personality and talk about your business.

According to Statista, people listen to podcasts for an average of 30 minutes and they offer a more personal way to reach potential customers.

People listen to them in the car, in the gym and while they're doing the cooking. Hearing you speak with enthusiasm about what matters to you helps build a closer connection.

Research by Radio Today found listeners tend to be younger; two-thirds are aged 16 to 34, and 23 per cent of people in the UK say they listened to one in the last month.

Listeners are likely to respond to adverts they hear. Of the 70 per cent who heard podcast advertising, three quarters took action as a result.

So if you're asked to be a podcast guest - say yes.

Or if there's a particular podcast host you'd like to work with, pop them a pitch over on e-mail.

Tell don't sell

Think about different angles that offer something useful for their listeners. Ideally your story will be emotional and relatable.

For example, Katie Tovey-Grindlay, founder of Woof Woof Network and Business Wonderland, also has a merchandise and events company called Crazy Dog Lady.

Her podcasts feature pet business owners, but rather than talk about what they do, they take listeners on a more personal journey and focus on their dogs (of course!)

Business advisor Heather Legge talks about how her Labrador Jetta helps her to relax.

Life coach Sandra Dawes shares how her rescue dog Lulu helped her cope with the death of her father.

It doesn't have to be a sob story, but you can see how sharing a little about your personal life is far more interesting.

Working with influencers

Like bloggers, we hear a lot about the importance of working with influencers.

As I've already discussed bloggers, I'm going to focus specifically on social media influencers, so pets or people with high numbers of social media followers.

As a pet business, your target audience is much more likely to follow other animals or pet writers than say, Katie Price or someone from Love Island, so it's a great way to raise awareness.

Similar to working with bloggers, do your research. Check their reputation and make sure they're the right fit for your brand. See who follows them and how engaged their audience is by examining likes, shares and comments.

Assess their content. Are the pictures of a decent quality? Do posts sound natural and authentic or are they simply taking a quick photo of a product and posting #ad.

If you see they've worked with another brand, there's no harm in contacting them and asking about their experience.

Sometimes influencers with smaller followings, known as micro-influencers, have a highly engaged audience.

One of my favourite accounts is @hazelandbramble. Jodie Forbes shares posts about her three dogs Hazel, Bramble and Tulip who do tricks, agility and dancing and have appeared at Crufts.

At the time of writing (August 2018) they had 1700 followers on Instagram.

I personally know the PR teams at Chuck It, Pit Pat and Natures Menu where they are brand ambassadors rate them very highly and see real value in working with them.

To explain a little more, I spoke to **Vicky Gunn from Millie's Beach Huts and Millie's Pet Services** (www.milliespetservices.co.uk) who has experience of working with bloggers and influencers.

Inspired by her gorgeous Springer Spaniel, Millie, she has a dog boutique which also offers a range of grooming services and her beach huts in Essex and Suffolk are used by parents and pawrents for days out.

How did you first come to work with a blogger?

Our very first guest to the beach huts was a blogger, though I hadn't booked her or planned it and I never had thought of working with one.

I found out on the morning she arrived and I'll admit that there was a bit of fear factor about it and I found myself constantly checking social media to see how her day was going. But she had a great time and produced a gorgeous blog afterwards.

She wasn't 'big' at the time. She had around 2,000 followers on Instagram and 1,000 on Facebook, but her blog was well read and she's now a massive blogger and vlogger over on Channel Mum, a website and online community for mums.

It was a nice experience. It didn't lead to a huge or immediate rise in bookings but I was able to put it on the front page of my website and provide social evidence that described the experience of using a beach hut.

Do you continue to work with bloggers?

Yes, every year I actively look for bloggers to visit my new beach huts because I recognise that people like to read about another person's experience (and a recent visit too).

I don't have children myself, so if a family wants to hire a hut but has some concerns around distance to toilets or the position of a hut, I can send them links to parenting blogger reviews and I find that they always convert to bookings.

I'd say that I don't use influencers with a view that they'll immediately result in their audience buying from me or following on social media.

My primary purpose for using influencers is because I need constant, fresh, social evidence which has a bit more depth than a photograph or a guest book entry.

Each of my thirteen beach huts has a day allocated for bloggers or vloggers every year.

What kind of response have you had from influencers who work purely on social media?

I find it takes time to see any impact with influencers on Instagram. Don't assume large numbers of followers will result in your own followers dramatically increasing.

I've had an influencer with 20,000 followers visit and didn't see a huge impact. You do have to work at making the most out of the coverage you get from them.

Think about commenting on and re-sharing their posts, photos and stories.

I personally think it can come down to whether that influencer will do their post and forget about you, or whether they have the business sense to think, 'It's been a year since I visited the beach hut, I'm going to revisit that post.'

What are the lessons you've learned?

I worked closely with three or four influencers over a longer period of time and find that those relationships have been the most beneficial.

Collectively we've built our social evidence, and now I get direct messages and queries though Instagram that I didn't before.

Also, I will now only work with micro influencers. An ideal person would have around 1000 to 3000 followers and I'd be looking for evidence that their values and brand are aligned with my own.

If I stuck my logo in the middle of their Instagram feed or blog, would it look out of place or fit right in?

I'm friends with many of the bloggers and find that we now refer opportunities between one another all the time.

It's all about building long term relationships and not assuming influencers are a quick fix to generating leads and sales.

If people write or post about me, planned or unplanned, I make a massive deal of it.

I always share it at the time and use it on my website and put it in my social media scheduler so it's seen again and again.

If they've taken the time to write about us, and I know how hard it is to consistently blog, I feel that I should take time to show that I value their efforts.

I blog myself and I think businesses should recognise that it's not simple, there is a skill and it's one to be appreciated.

What would your advice be to other businesses considering working with bloggers and influencers?

Do your research. Do they understand search engines and are their posts and headlines optimised? Or do they go for click bait titles, so their blogs will never be found by Google longer term?

See how many posts are just plugs and whether they are switching between brands all the time?

Warning signs would include an influencer who changes their dog's food constantly? If so, avoid them. Trust your gut feeling.

You want to work with people who have a genuine interest and passion for the companies they collaborate with. Micro influencers are more valuable and aligned to what I'm about.

Ask for their PR or media pack and this should have more than just their followers and Domain Authority or DA.

Ask for testimonials and conversion rates or evidence of the impact their campaign has had.

Look for someone who has engaged followers, in the UK and in the area of your business and with a similar audience.

For example, for our beach hut business, my target audience is aged between 26 to 44, in Essex and the outskirts of London.

A professional blogger or influencer will be able to provide this. If they can't, then it's a sign that they don't truly understand the impact of their efforts and you are unlikely to see that impact too.

CHAPTER SEVENTEEN

How having a famous pet can help your brand

♦ ♦ ♦

Chances are you have a pet if you have a pet business - and who doesn't love sharing photos of them being adorable?

While photos of your pet can be great for engagement, you might decide to give them their own account.

People warm to pets more than humans, and if you do this, you might find their account takes off far quicker than your own.

Thanks to Instagram, there's been a huge rise in pet influencers - adorable dogs, cats and all manner of animals - who represent brands as models and ambassadors rather than people.

Melody Lewis from PetLondon Models works with hundreds of su-paw-models and explains: "People feel more connected to animals on Instagram than any other platform and some are really famous. It's easier for an animal to get followers than a person.

"It's amazing how quickly these animals take off. People are thinking 'If I'm booking an animal for an advert, then maybe I should book a famous animal.'

"Just like with human models, if a pet already has a large social media following and is well known, it adds extra power to the campaign.

"Instagram has played a huge part in this as it's friendly and so easy for animals to go global. If you have a dog of a particular breed you can reach people all over the world."

If your pet becomes famous it makes your brand more visible.

To learn, I spoke with **Marianne de Fiouw, owner of Lilliput aka @little_London_maltese** about how her dog became global star.

With 137,000 followers on Instagram at the time of writing Lilliput is the most followed Maltese Terrier in the world.

She's worked on campaigns for LadBible, Now TV, River Island, Crufts, Good Housekeeping, the BBC, Warner Bros Attitude Magazine and has appeared in a video for - you guessed it - the Pet Shop Boys.

How did Lilliput's journey begin?

As a bit of a goof actually! A couple of friends with Maltese dogs set up pet Instagram accounts and I'd tease them about being juvenile, asking if they'd regressed to being 13 years old.

At that time I was completely ignorant of social media and barely even knew that Facebook wasn't available in hardcopy with paper pages!

I sat up and started paying attention when I saw how these individuals were able to connect with other Maltese dog families around the world and share their experiences and joy.

I realised it also meant I had a willing audience who wanted to hear about dogs and wouldn't ask me to change the topic of conversation once in a while!

I eventually admitted the error of my ways and set up an account for Lilliput.

Why do you think she's so popular?

I'd like to take all the credit and say it's down to Lilliput and me locking ourselves away and devising a sharp strategy which I expertly execute, but I'm afraid it's a lot simpler than that.

Lilliput's account has a strong content theme which stands out and leaves a lasting impression; she's an incorrigibly sassy yet vulnerable diva who is convinced she's the canine Kate Moss but is frequently embarrassed by her human pointing out that she's actually just a desperate wannabe raggamuffin.

People know what she's about and what to expect from her, which means they enjoy investing emotionally in her struggles to be recognised as the global icon she so plainly already is in her mind.

She's had a fair bit of publicity too - has this helped?

Yes definitely! It opens up her audience tremendously and goes some (small) way to making her a household name.

The Mail Online for example reaches 40 million people, so being on there really means you stand out from the many other pets.

Thousands are described as models despite never having been in front of anything other than an iPhone - and so wider publicity lends gravitas to the account.

It shows brands that you can attract publicity or interest which is what they're seeking for their own businesses.

What advice would you give to people who are trying to build their pet's profile?

Don't fixate on the numbers! And don't be tempted by short cuts. Instagram is replete with people who've bought followers and you can spot them every time.

Work on building your profile by engaging with accounts in which you're genuinely interested.

Leave personalised comments on posts you like and take the time to build relationships. Enjoy arranging occasional real life meet ups and sharing experiences and advice.

Try to create a clear identity for them and be consistent. If you can ensure you have a slight point of difference between yourself and the other cute pet accounts that'll also help attract like minded people to follow you.

It's a good idea to diversify your posts too, so you don't post the same things over and over again.

I think by now we've all seen the 'cute face, can I have more treats please?' post. Try to keep things different and interesting and invest in a decent camera.

It's not an overnight recipe for success but many Maltese accounts run in this sort of manner ,which started around the same time as Lilliput's, have since grown into the tens of thousands.

Perhaps most importantly, both the pet and the human have had so much fun with it along the way and forged some cherished friendships.

CHAPTER EIGHTEEN

Old fashioned PR - getting yourself out there!

♦ ♦ ♦

I've covered lots about having your business feature in newspapers, magazines, websites, social media, blogs and podcasts.

But there's so much to be said for old fashioned PR and physically getting your name, face and products under the noses of your ideal customer.

Dominic Hodgson (www.growyourpetbusinessfast.com) is a dog walker and trainer turned pet business coach and he agrees.

We met online - I'd written about a friend of his - and then in person at the North East Dog Festival in 2017.

He had a stall and was giving a dog training demo with his Cocker Spaniel Sid - so showing his expertise - and talking about his book, How To Be Your Dog's Superhero.

Being at an event in his local community proved to be a real eye opener, because while he was well known online, in real life it wasn't the case.

Dominic said: "On Facebook, everyone knows me. My posts get lots of likes and comments, but I was at an event in the North East which is where my business is based, and many people didn't know who I was.

"Don't get me wrong, I'm not the 'Don't you know who I am?' type of person but I thought I'd be recognised in my own community. It gave me a massive kick up the backside.

"It spurred me to be more visible and I contacted Living North, a lifestyle magazine, to see if they would feature my book and ended up doing a piece with them about how to fix some common dog training problems. This helped demonstrate my expert status.

"A lot of my communications strategy is e-mail marketing I'm on Facebook and I have a strong following but the experience made me see you need to show up in lots of different places so now on top of my pet business bootcamps, I focus on speaking at events, newsletters flyers, publicity and word of mouth."

Brilliantly, there are now dog shows and events taking place all over the country and, as Dominic says, they offer the chance for people to physically see you.

If you're a walker or sitter, you could have a stand with flyers, photos of dogs enjoying their walks and testimonials from clients. As a behaviourist, you could demonstrate the work you do.

An accessory or treat brand could show off their creations and give out samples, and if you're a pet photographer, using a selfie frame where you take photos of dogs then post them on your social media platforms would generate loads of sharable content and potential leads.

Another effective strategy is collaborating with businesses that complement what you do so have a brainstorming session and imaging the different places where pet owners go.

For example, if I go to the pub with my dog, I will happily pay through the nose for him to be happy and feel like he's having a treat too.

Our favourite pub is The Brandling Villa in Newcastle which we call the 'Dog pub' because it has a menu for dogs with ice cream, dog beer and Pawsecco.

They can choose from a chicken or beef Sunday Roast, sausage and eggs if it's breakfast time and Fillet O Frank - chicken on a bed of sausage and biscuits with gravy.

Yet week in week out I go to other dog friendly pubs who have nothing for dogs. Not even a biscuit tub or a gravy bone! I can't get my head around it.

There are so many independent bars and pubs now so if you sell biscuits and treats, why not call in and chat to the watering holes in your community?

If a dog knows they get a lovely treat when they go in their establishment, they're going to drag their owner in there every time they walk past.

Alternatively, if you make accessories, why not partner with a local gift shop, garden centre, cafe or even a clothes shop?

They take a cut of the profits but every sale makes people aware of your brand. And how often do you browse for gifts and buy something for yourself - or your dog?

It's about visibility and it's a really simple way to get your products in front of more people.

Paula Jardine makes pet accessories at The Eco Dog Design Company (www.ecodogdesigns.com) and has followed this strategy.

She set up her business after leaving a job in HR three years ago and shares the many ways she reaches her customers.

Can you tell me about the different ways you promote your brand?

Yes, our logo is on all our products and we're in retail outlets around the region such as dog groomers, dog cafes, dog day care centres, garden centres and gift shops.

I'm very active on social media - particularly Facebook, Twitter and Instagram - posting customer photos, behind the scenes and we have a Dog of the Month photo contest each month.

I attend shows all over the country and hand out cards to every customer and ensure each event has my website and social media on their social pages and vice versa.

As an eco-friendly brand we have a 'recycle and renew' scheme where customers can bring in an old collar so we can reuse buckles and clips in return for a discount on a new one.

My car is branded and on the back parcel shelf I have a display showing rows of my collars and the different patterns - it's a mobile shop window.

I monitor SEO on my website, register on all business directories and write newsletters and regular blogs where I link to other businesses or charities.

Finally, I support many charities, donating products to good causes and collaborate with other businesses, such as Ruffle Snuffle who make enrichment toys.

How does collaborating with outlets like cafes and garden centres help your business?

It helps spread the word and lets us ring the 'Eco Dog Design' bell and provides the opportunity for people to use these outlets as showcases.

Sometimes people will call and say, 'I've seen your products and would like to stock them at our store.'

I also use them as a hub for customers to buy online, and drop the items off at the locations so people don't have to pay postage.

This is great for the dog cafes, for example, as it means people usually stay for a coffee, so it benefits them too.

You've had some publicity as your Union Jack poo bag carrier featured in a Royal Wedding feature I did in the Sunday Mirror. What impact did this have?

We saw an increase in our social media followers and I did see a rise in orders for the Union Jack range!

I contacted the Sunday Mirror to see if I could use their masthead on my website and say, 'As seen in the Sunday Mirror,' and negotiated a fee of £150 as a small business.

I saw it as an investment in the long run as being featured in a national newspaper does build credibility in the market place.

You attend lots of shows and events. What lessons have you learned?

Events are a great way to find out what your customers like and inspire ideas. People ask about dog beds, Haltis and slip leads for example, and while at the moment I'm focusing on what I know I do well, these are things to consider in future.

Think outside the box when it comes to your audience. I've done really well by attending a horse show - many people with horses have dogs. Caravan shows have been a huge success too, so don't just focus on pet events.

CHAPTER NINETEEN

How to handle a crisis

♦ ♦ ♦

We're living in an age when we share every last cough, spit and splutter of our lives and brands want their customers to be shouting from the rooftops about them.

But what do you do when it's for the wrong reasons? Unfortunately, we're seven times more likely to share a negative experience than a positive experience online.

A few years ago a contact who works in the pet care industry called me. One of her clients claimed her dog had been returned home with a serious injury.

The client had shared photos and made serious claims about my contact on Facebook. The post had been shared hundreds of times and she was asking for my advice or what to do next.

I trust the person in question implicitly and believe there are two sides to every story - but her business and reputation were being destroyed online.

You can imagine her distress. The local newspaper had been in contact with her and a news agency for a response or 'right of reply.'

A right of reply is a practice where the journalist approaches a person or organisation when allegations of wrongdoing are being made about them and gives them the opportunity to make a comment before the story is published.

My contact had been offered this and had spoken to a solicitor who had put together a statement of what happened which was accurate but devoid of any emotion and sounded extremely defensive. As a journalist, I knew this would be disastrous for her reputation.

We reworked the statement so it remained accurate, but expressed how devastated they were by the dog's injuries and explained procedures had been put in place to ensure the safety of all animals. I contacted the local newspaper and news agency to ensure they used the revised statement.

Many clients came forward to support my contact and a few weeks later, she gave an interview to the local paper to reassure the community that lessons had been learned. Her business has recovered.

I don't want to scaremonger, but there may come a time when you're faced with a situation like this. Dogs can have accidents while out with walkers. Toys that have passed rigorous safety tests may injure a pet.

Stories spread like wildfire on social media and when you're caught in a storm it can be frightening so it helps to have an idea of how to react.

If an allegation is made about one of your products, or an animal that has been in your care, either on social media or to a publication, first and foremost, remain calm.

Can you speak to the person making the claim? Speaking to someone rather than responding on e-mail or direct message is far more likely to resolve or defuse a situation as they can express how they feel and you can empathise and tailor your response.

Have they made it in a social media post? If this is the case, try to take the conversation offline.

Comment on the post to say that you are investigating their allegation and ask to speak directly to them. Comment on any other comments to say you're investigating. It shows you care about your customers as you're addressing the situation and taking it seriously.

It's far worse not to acknowledge the allegation, so make an initial response as quickly as possible then investigate the claims they're making. Once you have all the facts, you can issue a more comprehensive statement.

This will cover what happened, why it happened and what steps you have taken to prevent it happening again. If an animal has come to harm, you should speak from the heart and be compassionate.

Don't issue a statement where you sound like a lawyer. Recall the product if you have safety concerns and make other customers aware of the situation. Finally, offer to pay the vet bill and apologise.

Put the statement on your website and on your social media pages - you can pin it to the top of your Facebook and Twitter page. Pause any scheduled social media updates until you feel confident the issue has been resolved.

You should know how to pause your social media updates already. This can be helpful at times when it might be inappropriate or insensitive to share scheduled posts.

Dorothy Perkins posted jolly tweets about having that #fridayfeeling the day after the Brexit Referendum which was deemed poorly timed given the nation was in turmoil.

If you are faced with a crisis, remember, we're all human and it will blow over and, unless something truly hideous has happened, you will find that friends and family and loyal customers who know how passionate you are about what you do will rally to support you.

CHAPTER TWENTY

Choosing the right PR

♦ ♦ ♦

Consumer spending on pets and pet related products has almost doubled in the last ten years in the UK, rising from £2.5 billion in 2007 to £4.6 billion in 2017 according to Statista.

Pets are part of the family and owners love showering them with gifts and affection, feeding them clean, nutritious food, taking them on luxury holidays, styling them in the most fashionable apparel and ensuring they're in peak condition.

So there is every chance your brand is going to be a huge success - it could be already.

You may be at the point where you know people like your brand, and more people want to experience it, and the more people who knew about it the greater your sales and reach could be.

If you've actioned all the advice I've given and you're at a crossroads where promoting your business is actually taking you away from what you do, and you want to scale your brand, then it might be time to call in a professional.

PR stands for Public Relations and a PR consultant will act as the middle man between you and the media.

They should have an understanding of the industry, a passion for what you do, and be brimming with ideas and contacts in the pet niche.

I'd recommend finding a firm local to you and perhaps start with a freelance consultant or small agency.

It's easy to be dazzled by big city PR firms - but bear in mind a smaller agency or one-man or woman band won't have the huge rent to pay and wage bills and this will reflect in the price. Plus, it's more personal and that's really important.

Some PR firms who look after pet brands also take care of their social media. If you've build up a following on your platforms and they're used to hearing your voice, this can be hard for someone to emulate, so think hard before doing this.

Collette Walsh is a media consultant to leading brands in the UK (www.collettewalshmedia.co.uk).

She's worked with Aldi on their pet range, The Vet Group and Webbox pet food and shares her advice on what to look for if you decide to hire a PR.

PR for a pet brand or entrepreneur isn't any old PR is it? Our pets are so special so what should entrepreneurs look for in a consultant or agency?

I'd recommend working with a freelance consultant or a small agency at the beginning as this is so much more personal than working with a larger organisation.

Choose one that recognises the bond we have with our pets. There are a few niche agencies out there, but if there isn't one local to you, ask for recommendations.

As you research, look at their social media and see if pets feature. If you spot an office dog, you know they will embrace your brand and shout about you from the rooftops!

Ask if they're worked with other pet brands or departments of a larger business, for instance, they may have worked with the pet department of John Lewis, so would have excellent connections.

Finally, are they immersed in the pet world? Do they get involved with things like the Family Pet Show or trade events like Crufts or Discover Dogs?

Are there specific skills or specialisms pet businesses need from a PR?

If your brand is a luxury item, maybe a bespoke dog bed, you need an agency with a good track record in promoting and placing luxury products. Look for agencies that specialise in Business to Consumer PR - known as B2C - with a good understanding of the lifestyle market.

If the appeal is broader, a pet food perhaps, chose an agency that is experienced in dealing with fast moving consumer brands. Ideally they will offer Business to Business or B2B PR with contacts at trade titles too.

Appearing in trade publications makes the industry aware of your name and product and can draw investment in future. One day you may even consider selling your business and potential investors will want to see your brand in the consumer and trade press.

What questions should pet entrepreneurs ask potential PRs?

Ask where they would propose to place stories. PR consultants or agencies won't give the names of their contacts but they should be able to tell you the titles where they think your brand would fit and where they have a good working relationship with journalists.

With a larger PR agency, ask if they have a journalist database subscription. This may mean you pay a little more, but journalists move around a lot and if they have this, you can feel reassured they have access to contacts that are updated daily.

Do they have a media monitoring service that keeps track of their mentions in print, online and social media?

Again, this will be more expensive but this facility is useful for looking at cuttings and coverage.

Ask if they provide a monthly report or coverage book - this will be helpful to refer to and enables you to see if you're getting return on investment (ROI).

How do PRs demonstrate ROI?

A lot of people think it's about sales but it's more about AVE which is Advertising Value Equivalent. PR is difficult to quantify but AVE helps you understand what a piece of coverage would cost in terms of advertising for the same amount of space.

So for example, a full page advert in a pet magazine might cost £2000. If you pay your PR £1000 a month and they place a full page feature in the magazine about your product that's an excellent investment as editorial is far more likely to influence a buying decision.

Clients need to understand how they will quantify return on investment. It's not just about being on TV or in the Daily Mail - these are golden moments but there's the day to day coverage that PRs work hard to secure too and you need to see what is of value and which pieces of coverage prompt people to pick up the phone or go online and order.

I've worked with clients who are very keen for website links to be included but you can't insist on this can you?

No, it's of no value to the publication to give links and a lot of the national newspapers in the UK have stopped putting in backlinks.

They see it as advertising revenue they're missing out on and you risk damaging a relationship with a reporter if you insist they include them.

I always include a client's website address in my press releases but I tell them if it's taken out, there is nothing I can do. If it gets in, see it as a bonus.

Ultimately as long as your brand is mentioned and your name as the creative or business owner, people will Google you and find you and that's how you can track and source the impact of your coverage.

How often should they be communicating with their PR?

I like to have a check in every week with bullet points on any coverage achieved and what is being worked on in the week ahead. This is a brief e-mail.

When I first start working with clients, we meet face to face so I can really get a feel of the brand and after this we have a monthly call.

Remember your PR is a professional just like a lawyer or an accountant and you want their time to be spent effectively.

Is there anything else pet entrepreneurs should consider?

Yes, my final piece of advice it to be patient. Results don't come through for the first six months. The first three months is about building a relationship with a client and the journalists you hope will write about them. You need to commit to a time frame and I would suggest a year.

Then, take time to reflect what you've achieved by analysing the coverage you've had, your growth and mentions on social media and how your business has evolved. Pet entrepreneurs are achieving great things and with the right support, you can join them.

THE FINAL WORD

I hope you've found this book helpful. The idea to write it came from having many conversations with business owners over the years about how to get publicity.

Many of them approached me after spending thousands of pounds on expensive PR companies and achieving very little.

Please don't think I'm knocking PRs as there are so many brilliant firms out there, but when you're starting out as a pet entrepreneur, every penny counts.

The advice I've shared is everything I've learned in two decades as a journalist and will give you everything you need to start publicising your business.

I truly hope further down the line, like many of the start ups I've spoken to over the years, you'll be hiring a fantastic PR to scale your brand and go HUGE!

I'd love to hear about your 'wins' so if you've read the book, followed the advice and had a story published, please share it with me!

You can join my Facebook group where I'll be sharing tips, journalist requests and inspiring stories of people who have succeeding in securing publicity at: www.facebook.com/groups/publicitytipsforpetbusinesses/

Following on from this book, I've launched a new website, www.publicityforpetbusinesses.co.uk, where you'll find regular blog posts and advice on creating content, promoting your business and working with the media.

You can find my journalism website featuring stories from the pet world at www.rachelspencerwrites.com

You can follow my pet blog www.thepawpost.co.uk where I share posts about people in the pet world, inspiring animals, product reviews and travel features.

I also work with individuals and brands on a one to one basis as a consultant.

If you'd like to work with me, I'd love to hear from you, so e-mail me at Rachel@rachelspencerwrites.com.

ABOUT THE AUTHOR

Rachel Spencer is a freelance journalist who specialises in writing about animals and the pet industry.

She's written pet articles for a wide range of publications including The Daily Mail, The Mail on Sunday, The Independent, The Sunday Mirror, The Sunday Express, The People, The Sun, Asda Good Living, Closer magazine, Real People magazine, Love It! magazine and BuzzFeed.

A dog obsessive, in 2017 Rachel decided to set up a pet blog www.thepawpost.co.uk, so she could write even more pet stories and it featured in Vuelio's Top 10 Pet Blogs of 2017 and 2018.

She lives in Newcastle-upon-Tyne with her boyfriend Tommy and her terrier cross Patch.

ACKNOWLEDGEMENTS

The idea for writing this book came during a chat I had with the brilliant Katie Tovey Grindlay of Woof Woof Network and Business Wonderland when I started my blog in 2017.

I was gushing about how happy writing pet stories made me and she said, 'You should write a book.' I never thought I could actually do it!

But it's the people in the stories that makes my work so rewarding and there are two very remarkable ladies in this book that deserve a special mention. Every time I write about them it makes me cry.

Liz Haslam from Beds For Bullies first broke me in 2013 when I interviewed her for an article on Bait Dogs - innocent, helpless pets used as bait in dog fights. We stayed in touch and I can't express how much I admire the work she does. So thank you Liz for helping me find my way into my niche as a pet journalist.

Jade Statt from StreetVet called me out of the blue in 2017 to see if I'd write about her work helping homeless dog and their owners. We met and I spent a day shadowing her for a feature for my blog. Again, her kindness and compassion blew me away. What Jade and her team do is so humbling.

Liz and Jade care for the forgotten dogs. Some of their stories are horrible. People don't want to read about them or acknowledge that such awful things happen. I feel honoured to know them. They give you faith in human nature.

On a lighter note, I'm very appreciative to my experts Rosie Robinson, Gareth Dunning, Jane Common and Collette Walsh who have shared their knowledge with you.

Thanks to the business owners and people who have talked about their experience in the media; Katie from Business Wonderland, Vicky Gunn from Millie's Beach Huts, Marianne Di Fiouw who owns Lilliput the Maltese, Paula Jardine of the Eco Dog Design Company, dog photographer Kerry Jordan, and dog trainer and business coach Dominic Hodgson. I hope as a pet entrepreneur their insights are both helpful and inspiring.

I'm grateful to my friends in the industry who have listened to me stressing and given me encouragement and reassurance. To Helen, my blogging buddy for keeping me sane and telling me I was doing the right thing, Suzanne, my old Warrington Guardian colleague who has the patience of a saint, Alice, who told me I COULD write a book because she did it and to Jane for her meticulous attention to detail.

Huge thanks to my poor, poor boyfriend Tommy for putting up with a very stressed girlfriend and for knowing when to bring me a glass of wine or chocolate bar or when to make a sharp exit.

Big cuddles and stinky kisses to our lovely boy Patch, a lively terrier who we adopted just as I started this book and who has enjoyed lots of walks as I tried to get my creative juices flowing!

But most of all, to my gorgeous, funny, fiesty, brave and beautiful girl Daisy, my dog of nine years who we sadly lost in April 2018.

She turned me into the crazy dog lady I am today. We miss her so much and she is forever in our hearts.

THANK YOU!

Thank You for reading **Publicity Tips for Pet Businesses**

If you enjoyed this book, I would really appreciate it if you would consider leaving a review of this book, no matter how short, at the retailer site where you bought your copy or on sites like Goodreads.

You are the key to this book's success.

I read every review and they really do make a huge difference.

Reviews help other readers to discover the kind of books they want to read and writing them is a great way to support authors.

Printed in Great Britain
by Amazon